ARE YOU READY FOR PAID ADS?

How To Get Your Business Ready For Massive Growth

SILVIA COLETTO

Cover image by: Silvia Coletto
Book design by: SWATT Books Ltd

Printed in the United Kingdom
First Printing, 2021

ISBN: 978-1-3999-0925-9 (Paperback)
ISBN: 978-1-3999-0926-6 (eBook)

Silvia Coletto
Northampton

www.paidadsschool.com

To Mum, Dad, and Levi
who believed in me
way before I believed in myself.

Table of Contents

Introduction

One night in late August 2020 I was in Leamington Spa for an after-hours networking session.

It was my first (and also last) face to face networking meeting after covid, before the UK went back into lockdown number two.

I had big news for the room. I had recently started my own business, so I spent the entire meeting talking about the amazing things paid advertising can do for companies of (almost) any shape and size.

Something did not feel right though, and as soon as the meeting ended, I found out why.

One of the business owners approached me, sat down with his drink, and asked me if I could be more specific about what I meant by paid advertising. He thought he had a pretty good idea, but he just wanted to double check. He was hoping I could spare a few minutes to clarify.

That floored me. I was so wrapped up in the excitement I forgot the basics, and simply assumed everyone knew what I was talking about.

I consciously made an effort to strip the explanation down to the raw, essential fundamentals so that a kid could easily understand it.

By the end of it he said, “You should teach these things. It is valuable information, you made it really simple, and I bet there are many business owners like me out there, who don’t know how to use paid advertising to grow.”

I laughed out loud. Me?! Teaching people what?! No way! I genuinely thought what I said was nothing special or groundbreaking. Surely there were way more qualified and experienced professionals out there?

I brushed the idea off for a few months. But then, more and more people I regularly networked with told me I should either write a book or at least create a course, and yet, I still did not believe I was qualified enough. Impostor syndrome surely did a number on me on this one!

That changed the day a dear friend of mine asked if I could teach his daughter in law how to set up and run her own Facebook advertising Christmas campaign. Going through that experience with her opened my eyes.

I was clear, I was concise, I didn't use any jargon, and I backed up any recommendations with the reason why it needed to be done in that specific way. Even better, I reframed expectations and explained where paid advertising fits in the marketing ecosystem and how it is just one piece of the puzzle, instead of the magical sales machine most people think it is.

She is now running successful e-commerce campaigns to this day, and I used that experience to create my own Facebook Advertising course for beginners, which then gave me the inspiration to write the guide you have in your hands right now.

If you are a business owner, a marketing director, or a decision maker who is looking to get a better understanding of paid advertising overall, without having to lose valuable time and money by having to run the advertising accounts by yourself, then you're in the right place.

If, on top of that, you have little time to dedicate to this, and want a read that's non-technical and to the point, you will be able to breeze through this less than no time at all.

Ready to get stuck in? Let's go!

1

Beware of the 'Fingers Crossed Strategy'

Paid advertising can be defined as any form of advertising that a company spends money to run. Nowadays, paid advertising is mostly online-based and is commonly considered the opposite of organic marketing – a group of promotional activities businesses label as 'free'.

Quite a deceiving label, if you ask me, because although you're not directly buying clicks or impressions, you are still spending company time and resources (sometimes too much time or resources) for the return that you get.

With paid advertising, you are effectively renting space on a platform which your target audience spends time on, so you can reach the people who are most likely to be interested in your product or service.

Ads come in different shapes and sizes, such as:

Display Ads

Ever gone on a website, looked at a pair of shoes, and suddenly, you see the same shoes everywhere you go on the internet? Yep, THOSE ads.

Search Ads

When you search for something on Google, the top 3 or 4 results are paid for. Those ads show up there because advertisers bid on keywords similar to the ones you typed in to find those results. The more relevant the ad, the cheaper it becomes, and the more likely it is to occupy one of these coveted spots.

Social Ads

These are the social media version of Display Ads. Instead of showing you an ad based on what you are searching for, social ads work on demographics and interests. So, if the advertiser knows their audience is, for example, 30-65, female, living in London and a parent of teens, they can show ads exclusively to this customer profile.

Remarketing Ads

You can show these ads to people who have already visited your website but not bought or inquired with you. You can also use remarketing ads to upsell existing customers, especially in the case of e-commerce brands, where you are able to customise the products people see based on what they've already purchased. Amazon is the undisputed master at this.

In other words? Paid advertising can follow your customers literally *everywhere* around the internet until they are ready to buy from you (although I wouldn't suggest the blanket approach – that's the fastest way for customers to get fed up with you!).

Always remember that only 3% of your visitors on average are ready to buy or inquire on their first visit. The other 97% are not quite ready yet, which means you have to nurture those visitors down the funnel, through a few more steps in the customer's journey.

Your aim is for those visitors to get to know and trust you, so that when the time comes, they'll be more likely to choose you.

The next logical thing you might be asking at this point is, what is required to run ads and what ads should I be running?

First things first. If you force yourself to get into paid ads without making sure that your business is ready for it, then you are in for a disaster. And I am not exaggerating.

People who do not understand ads tend to believe that spending money on ads will surely generate money one way or another. This is true only if the work is done properly. Otherwise, you are just burning cash to feed agencies that will gladly tell you everything you want to hear, as long as they get their paycheck at the end of the month.

That's why, when I founded the Paid Ads School, I swore to put transparency above everything else. If I determine that you're not ready for paid ads, I will let you know. I do not ever want to spend money unnecessarily if I know that it will get you nowhere.

On the other hand, if your business is ready to run paid ads, then expect me to put my all into it. Sugarcoating is not my style. I am not interested in empty promises, but proactive decisions based on data.

Data is an obsession for me, in fact, I feel that I need to take you on a little trip down memory lane to explain how I got to this point. Otherwise, it will not make much sense to you why I do what I do, the way that I do it.

The first years of my life were spent in a small village of ex-farmers in northwestern Italy, close to the border with Slovenia and Austria.

Now, I definitely was not some kind of genius who started talking about marketing and advertising at a very young age (although it would have been prophetic if I had).

On top of that, for the first 28 or so years of my life, I was also an extremely shy and introverted person (I still am, but not as much!). Could be because I was an only child, could be because I literally was the only kid in my extended family. Either way, like a lot of you, I grew up feeling like the proverbial 'outsider'.

My introversion was not the only thing that made my childhood challenging. In fact, I would say being a stickler for detail was my biggest problem. I am not sure if it was the influence of the adults around me, or if it was just who I was, but everything — and I mean *everything* — had to be done in a specific way. I liked control, structure, and order. Hardly a good way to make friends with kids who made a mess everywhere they went, and naturally so. Maybe some of you can relate?

Fast forward a few years and I entered high school. The highlight of these 5 years was being constantly reminded that I was awful at anything even remotely scientific. The best I could hope for, they concluded, was to become a librarian, because 'reading was definitely my thing'.

So, like the obedient teenager that I was, I accepted what I was told, did not question a thing, and believed that a librarian was all I could ever aspire to become.

High school went by in a flash, and I soon found myself travelling 300 miles away from home to go to the university of Pisa to study Publishing. Little did I know that my life was about to change.

Not long after entering university, thanks to my boyfriend at the time, I got introduced to the business world. Shadowing their salespeople, I was able to get some field experience. I travelled multiple times to France and Switzerland. Not only was that a valuable experience I would have never gotten from university, but it also made me realise that what I was told I should become was nowhere near what I was actually good at.

And so, after graduating and getting my Bachelor's degree in Publishing, I went to Milan to get a Master's degree in Business Administration, followed by an internship in what is now the biggest PR and communications company in the world, Burson Cohn & Wolfe.

I did my first internship with them for 9 months before going to work for a financial PR company. One day, a colleague told me one of his connections on LinkedIn from Milton Keynes, UK, was looking to hire an Italian with good English to work full time as a translator, as their marketing agency had lots of Italian clients.

Two weeks later, I had my interview. Another two weeks after that, I boarded a one-way flight to the United Kingdom and have never looked back.

That was October 2014.

With no family and friends to help me out, it was the best time to learn how to be independent. In the five years that followed, I worked for another marketing company, a car dealer group, and I had the privilege to help get a startup off the ground (now the uber-successful guys at Armchair Marketing), while at the same time learning the ropes of paid advertising.

After what I can only describe as priceless startup experience, I went back into the corporate world leading the paid acquisition department for an international fleet management company. Alongside that, I started my own company, called the Paid Ads School.

Why did I stick with paid ads out of all the marketing specialties I could have chosen? It is simple. It is just too good of a skill to let go. Plus, it satisfies the inner child in me who loves to follow a structure. I get to look at numbers, formulas and Excel sheets every day, which in my world, is nothing short of paradise. It is just funny how my teachers would have sworn numbers were never going to be my thing, when now, it is all I do for a living these days.

Why am I telling you all this again?

I wanted to give you a little insight of how my life took a full U-turn, and how I went from being a kid with OCD tendencies to using the same obsession for detail to fuel a successful advertising agency.

I also realised that my experience growing up and what happens in the paid ads arena these days is scarily similar.

Just like I was repeatedly told that I could only be a librarian, business owners are told there is only one way to run paid ads, and there is only one number they should pay attention to in order to judge successful advertising: revenue.

That couldn't be further from the truth, especially in B2B spaces. The role of advertising is not to sell.

Read it again.

The role of advertising is not to sell. Otherwise, what are you even paying your sales team for?

The role of advertising is to bring as many highly targeted eyeballs as possible to your product or service on autopilot, so that the likelihood they will eventually convert to a sale increases exponentially.

Because that is what you're hoping ads will do for you, right? Growth. You're likely standing at the crossroads, knowing that it is time to scale your business faster than you have ever done before, wondering how you should go about doing that.

If you are not running ads, then you are most likely getting your inquiries from referrals and networking. Which are great, do not get me wrong, but they can be hit and miss. There are times when you receive a streak of great referrals, and there are times when you will go for months without one, which is something you cannot afford. Whatever business you have, scaling successfully requires a consistent flow of inquiries and a predictability in how many you are going to close.

Seeing that you are reading this book right now, you have probably heard that doing paid advertising is a great way to scale faster. The problem is, how? You have no idea how it works, right?

Before you hit that search button looking for someone to run ads for you, first things first. Are you even ready?

Here are some signs that you *might* not be ready for paid ads (yet!):

- You don't know exactly who your client is
- You cannot accurately describe your customer's buyer journey
- You do not have a defined offer
- You do not know what you want your ads to achieve
- You do not have a complete sales funnel
- You do not know your numbers
- You are expecting instant results
- You are not making any organic sales
- Your website is not mobile responsive
- Enquiries drop into an unmonitored inbox
- You do not have a "Click to Call" number on every page of your website
- You do not have Google Analytics installed
- Your website is not managed by you or your team (or at least a very close third party)
- You do not have conversion tracking installed

- You are not present or consistent where your customers are spending their time

If you go through this list and determine you are not ready, it's time to speak to me (you will find my contact details at the end of this book).

If you determine you're ready, in most cases, it will go like this:

"Let me see what's out there" you think as you open your browser and type in *'best paid advertising agencies near me'*. Now you have several pages of search results for paid advertising agencies, and you start your research reading reviews and testimonials, and digging into their social media accounts.

As you dig deeper, you ask more questions. What does a good advertising agency do? What questions should I ask an advertising agency before hiring them?

To help you reach a decision, you are probably going to ask other businesses what agency they use and if they are any good. However, unless they have advanced knowledge of paid advertising, they will not be able to give you accurate information, just feelings.

Most businesses cross their fingers and just hope they hired a good agency. That is what I call the 'Fingers Crossed Strategy'.

You just cross your fingers and hope that you are in the hands of someone who knows what they are doing, because you sure as hell do not – hence why you are looking for some help. At the end of the day, you are in business to do what you love, not to run paid ads.

And while there are great advertising agencies out there who truly care for their clients, there are also agencies who are all about the money. So let me show you what these agencies look like.

Most of these agencies will not explain in detail what they're going to do for you. They will omit as much information as possible so that further down the line, they can twist the situation to their own advantage.

If you do not meet an agency like that, you are probably going to talk to one that promises a certain number of inquiries from month one, even though they do not know enough about your business to be able to make that promise.

You can sit through as many meetings as you want with these two types of agencies, but it is very unlikely either will be honest and straightforward enough to tell you "We don't have the answers for you right now, but we can find out the answers by looking through your data."

This type of agency does not try to hide things from you and does not promise you anything just to get you to swipe your credit card. This is the kind of honesty that you deserve. They will ask you questions such as:

- What services does your business provide?
- What are the services that your business is prioritizing right now?
- How much do these services cost?
- How much profit do you get from them?
- What are your short-term and long-term goals?
- What is your average conversion rate?
- If you worked with an agency before, what did you like and what did you not like from that experience?
- Do you have any active marketing projects right now?
- What is your budget for those marketing activities?
- How much are you making from these marketing efforts?
- Who are your competitors and are they doing something we should be aware of?
- What specific locations do you want to run the ads in?
- What goal do you want to achieve from these ads?
- Who are your target customers?
- Are there any specific inquiries you don't want to get?
- If you can wave your magic wand, in 12 months, what does success look like to you?
- When you receive an inquiry, where does it go and who handles it?
- What process do you have when dealing with inquiries?
- Do you have a website?

- Do you have any way to track traffic and sales on your website?

Not all questions will be relevant to your specific case, but for the ones who are, it is vital you answer with honesty and clarity. Sometimes that means you might realise you do not have the answers, and you need to go find them before you move forward. That is absolutely normal, and not a problem.

If you tried to guess any of these answers on the spot, the agency would not get a clear picture of what your business looks like right now, which in turn means you would not get the best advice anyway, so why even waste your time and money?

Now, in comparison to the two agencies described earlier on, that either promised you everything or did not promise anything at all, don't these people already sound like they know their stuff?

The rule of thumb is, if an agency claims anything that seems too good to be true, then it probably *is* too good to be true. If you are only spending £3,000 per month, it makes sense for you to not believe promises of hundreds of thousands of pounds in sales.

I know you are going to want and need more specifics than this, and I've got you. We will dive right into the heart of paid advertising, the ins and outs, the do's and don'ts, and I will make sure that once you are done with this book, you will be more confident in understanding how ads work for your business and how to make sure that you have got the right people to help you.

2

Know your buyers' journey like the back of your hand

As I have already mentioned in chapter one, paid advertising finds the highest possible number of quality people to introduce to your business. What most business owners or key decision makers think instead, though, is that ads should generate immediate sales.

I will never stop repeating this: the role of paid ads is not to make sales. If it does happen, that is a bonus, but fixating on the equivalence 'ads=sales' is an extremely dangerous misconception.

Saying that your goal is to make more sales is not even remotely clear or specific enough, which means it is very unlikely to give you the results you expect.

How do you get to that sale? What are the steps your prospect needs to take? What are the milestones you need to hit first? Ads are just one of the many touch points along the buyer journey.

Have you heard that it takes an average of seven touch points to make a sale? This alone should tell you that a single ad is unlikely to immediately make people want to buy from you. An ad is supposed to spark interest, and with enough interest, the potential customer will continue their buyer journey towards the actual sale later down the line.

Although yes, I get it. Advertising agencies often market ads as a surefire way to spectacular revenue growth. This approach is so common most decision makers have now associated paid advertising with getting immediate sales. I suspect you could be one of them too?

It is in your best interest to reprogram that mindset and understand that running ads is only one of the many steps you need to take. There are no shortcuts. You need to have a good understanding of the whole journey your prospect is going to go through before buying from you. New visitors who make an immediate purchase, especially in B2B relationships, are rare.

The good news is, we have all been buyers at some point. You know what you do as a buyer, so just dig into that. Put yourself in the buyer's shoes. How would you usually get to that purchase decision? How long does it usually take for you to decide to buy? What questions do you usually ask? Let's quickly dive into a customer's purchase journey with an easy example.

Let's say you want to buy a car. What is the first thing that you are going to do? The specifics differ from one person to another, but most people would hit up Google and see what cars are available right now, check different cars in their price range, go to comparison websites to see which car fits in their budget, and then check out reviews for those cars.

The buyer does not really reach a solid decision at this point and will usually have two cars in mind that are equally as good, which means it comes down to what deals are out there. With those options in mind, they look for reviews and see what current owners have to say. Still indecisive, they check out different dealerships near them to see which one will offer them the best price and packages.

It does not usually end there either. Friends and their family's opinions might be factored in too. Still undecided, especially since it is a big purchase, they would take their top options for a test drive, and once they find the car they really want, they go through that journey of deciding which dealership they want to get it from.

Sellers often think that when someone visits their website, the visit will turn immediately into a sale, or at least an inquiry. But if you put yourself in your customer's shoes, and think of the whole process they go through, then you would realise that it's not that simple. In fact, as I have already mentioned in chapter one, only 3% of your visitors are ready to make a purchase. This means that most of your visitors are interested but not yet ready to buy.

This is the same for every industry. The touchpoints may vary, the percentage may vary, but the principle is the same. Being able to understand your buyer's journey, will help you guide them properly and turn mere visitors into real sales.

So, what are you going to do with this hefty 97% of people left? Keep showing in front of them with value. Do not let them forget that your business is there for them, so that they can keep you in their list of businesses to contact once they are ready to purchase.

Now let us presume that you have now gone back to review and map your customer journey, and you know exactly who you are talking to, what problems they have, how you can help them get to their new desired state, and what the journey to take them from point A to point B looks like. You are now ready to discuss the next step, namely, what ad strategy fits the goal you're trying to achieve.

The average business owner does not realize how many things they can do with paid advertising. Here are some examples:

- Get more signups to your webinar
- Get more subscribers for your newsletter
- Schedule more discovery calls
- Get more inquiries
- Get more demo requests
- Have more people check out Google maps for directions to come to your store

However, before you start paying agencies to try multiple things at a time, sit down first and let us discuss your priorities.

Now I am sure that you would love to go all guns blazing and get those inquiries through every channel known to man, but it doesn't really work that way, and it could be counterproductive. In advertising (but the same can be said for marketing in general), it is dangerous to chase all the shiny things and launch multiple campaigns at once. You first have to make one of your goals a priority – and may I add, make sure it is realistic!

What is your business most focused on now? It is hard enough to get off the ground one campaign at a time, so believe me when I say it is going to be a wild mess if you blast a ton of ads out and just hope for the best. You are going to end up turning yourself into one of those annoying companies that you once put in your spam list.

So first, gather up those numbers and think about the most important outcome you want from your ads. If you want more signups for your webinar, how many? Do they have to be from a specific industry? Any specific location? Any specific demographic?

The more detailed you are with the objectives, the more likely you are to find the best audience and the best results.

If you already run ads that are not working the way you want them to work, then it is probably due to either lack of clarity on what you want, or some basics not being in place (more on those in the following chapters).

Lack of clarity is an especially tough one. If you are not clear on the goal, or unsure whether it is even realistic, you run the risk of having an agency completely miss the mark. Which then translates into running ads that do not get you anywhere. You lose money and you are still confused as to why. So, be sure that you are crystal clear on what you want, and be even more crystal clear while explaining that to your chosen advertising partner.

Let me get this out there again for the third time: paid ads are not your magical solution to get sales. They are only one of the several touch points in your customer's journey. Stay away from the people who tell you that pushing out ads is a surefire way to make money.

Having said that, paid ads are still a crucial step in getting in front of a lot of brand new potential customers.

Through a properly executed ad campaign, you can reach hundreds of thousands of clients/customers/buyers, even millions if your budget allows. Make sure to nurture all the inquiries you get, because – well – you paid for them. And before you know it, *bam!* You will make more sales as a result.

3

It's all about the numbers

When is the right time for your business to run paid ads? Well, as usual, it depends.

It is likely not a good idea to spend money on ads when you have just started your business (unless you have received investment and the investors are mandating a certain amount is spent on ads).

How about when you have just created a brand new product or service and you are eager for everyone to know about it? Or maybe when you have hired one or two employees? Hmm, still not quite there?

Usually, the best time to step into paid advertising is when you are already making consistent sales of whatever you are looking to advertise. And I'm not talking about 1, or 5, or 10 or even 20 sales. You need to have an already well-established product or service, as well as well-oiled internal processes. Otherwise what is the point in paying to get inquiries, only to burn them because you gave them a bad experience?

Believe me when I say that advertising your business before you have your processes covered is committing marketing suicide.

So first, make sure that your product or service works. Second, make sure that your processes have been well thought-out to the point that you would love to be a customer of your own business. Remember that advertising means exposing your business to scrutiny from hundreds or thousands of people. What would they see? Do you have your best cards ready? You would not want to mess it up badly enough for people to purposely avoid doing business with you.

It does not matter if you pay an advertising agency millions to advertise your products and services. If your products (or how you present them) are not working, they will not sell. If you are getting consistent sales, however, this is a sign you're going in the right direction. Especially if your customers are making repeat purchases.

Let us say that you are in this exact situation right now and you are ready to get started. The next question that you are likely going to have is, how much should I spend? Without fail, every customer who wanted to run ads has asked me this question. And I usually answer with, "How long is a piece of string?"

It would be very hard, if not impossible, for me to say how much you should spend until I understand your business properly. If you just want an idea, the very minimum you should set aside to start *testing* ads and campaigns is around £500 per month. And this is *only* if you are a small business that genuinely has no other budget available. If you think you can't afford to spend £500 a month on advertising, then you are likely not ready yet.

I always say as a rule of thumb, when it comes to advertising (or marketing in general), only spend money that you are comfortable losing. If you think that you will not go broke if you dish out that £500, then yes, you can start talking about ads.

At this point the first thing I would ask you if I sat down with you face to face, would be to tell me what is the number one priority for your business right now (remember chapter two?). If you are not sure what the priority is, then I would have to keep asking probing questions until we get to the bottom of it, because again, no clear goal equals no results you will end up being happy with. We need to start with your number one priority.

Next, I would ask you how much you're selling your top priority product/service for, and how much profit you make from it. Next, what is the conversion rate of your sales team? If you get 10 inquiries, how many of these will turn into a sale?

These are all extremely important questions. Not because I'm nosey, but because it will tell me how much you can afford to pay right now for a single inquiry before your ads become unprofitable.

Say your product is £1,000, and your fixed cost is £200. Your profit per sale is £800, and you have a 20% conversion rate (1 in 5). Divide £800 (profit) by five, and you get £160. Now make this calculation using your own numbers to find your maximum cost per inquiry.

In this example, £160 is the maximum amount that you should be looking to pay for a single inquiry before running ads starts to become unprofitable.

I am not saying that the moment you spent £161 on a single inquiry you would have to turn the ads off; £160 is the benchmark you did not have before, that guides you in the decision of sticking with a campaign or going back to the drawing board.

Ongoing communication between the advertising people and your business then means that if the conversion rate changes, or the profit changes, new calculations must be made, and that calculation becomes the new benchmark.

Now hear me out here. These numbers become a lot less tight if you sell high-value products or services, or if your model is based on repeat business (such as memberships or subscriptions, to name just a couple).

Great customer service also helps to sway one-off customers. How many of them will refer other customers to you? If you nurture and treat these customers correctly, they will keep supporting you one way or another, and suddenly, the £160 you spent on getting an inquiry starts to feel like a small change in comparison to how much profit you are getting from them.

That is why you should consider, whenever and if at all possible, the lifetime value of your customer. This way, you are not tying yourself down to a lower (and sometimes extremely hard to achieve) cost per inquiry.

As a rule of thumb:

- One-off customer: stick to the cost per inquiry you calculated earlier
- Recurring customer: calculate their lifetime value and use it to guide the decision of how much more you can spend to acquire one

This should go without saying, but if you are exponentially going over that £160 (again, this number is only for our specific example), then that means something is not right. At that point, consider turning off the ad campaign or reducing the spend while you find out the root of the problem.

Never spend money just for the sake of spending money. This is one of the things that frustrates me the most when looking at fellow paid advertising people. These agencies work off a monthly budget and make a point to spend it all. Some of them don't bat an eye at the results (or lack thereof), as long as they get their management fee at the end of the month. They deliver you a report, and you respond with, "But this isn't what we were aiming towards this month." Response? "Apologies. We will make the changes and try again next month."

This cycle would continue for as long as they can drag it out, even though the decent thing to do here would be to be honest and say that something is not working, and that the ads have to be turned off or spend has to be reduced until the problem is found and fixed. Do not be a victim to these agencies and know when it is time to put your foot down.

Now that we have talked about the numbers, how to know your cost per inquiry, and how important thinking in terms of lifetime value is, let us quickly talk about your sales process.

This is crucial, and as I have already mentioned earlier in this chapter, whatever process you have will determine how good or bad the customer experience is. This, in turn, can make or break a sale, and can also affect your customer retention.

I usually try to figure out if my client's business has a solid sales funnel by asking them to tell me how they handle an inquiry, or how they upsell someone who bought from their website directly. From the moment a customer fills out a form, to what email it goes to, to who picks up the enquiry and how fast, to how many times they follow up, etc. If they are unable to run through the whole process with ease, then it usually means that whatever they are doing is not watertight.

This is a common problem, and most businesses struggle with it. It doesn't matter how complicated the sales funnel is. In fact, the easier the better. The important thing is that it is secure, it is working, and that a customer will not get lost along the way. Otherwise, we are just pouring all these inquiries into a funnel that is full of holes.

I remember back in 2015, while working in the automotive industry, our marketing team was getting a lot of heat from dealerships that were adamant they were not getting any inquiries from us. We knew it was not possible because the data said otherwise; we eventually found out that the enquiries were dropped into an unmonitored inbox, not picked up by the sales team in time, and therefore lost.

Mistakes like this one could cost you a great deal of money, and a huge sigh of discomfort as you try to calculate how many sales you could have closed if only your process did not look like a gruyere cheese.

So, one piece of advice. Go check your sales funnel right now and make sure all things fall in place correctly, all channels where an inquiry could go to are monitored, and that there are no dead branches in the process like an unmonitored inbox with hundreds of unread inquiries.

Best of luck! And remember that I am here for you!

4

Build an inquiry-friendly website

Your website is your most important digital asset. Some people may disagree, but I will defend this statement to my last breath.

There are professionals who believe it is possible to run a business without a website; they say, you can just use social media and still make money. Sure, it is possible, but just because it is possible, this doesn't mean that it is the best thing to do. In my opinion, building a business on borrowed land is not the smartest move.

What if any of your social accounts gets hacked or suspended? Will the business stop running then? It is a common thing for Facebook and Instagram to suspend accounts these days, and at times it happens for no apparent reason. Rules change all the time. Sometimes, it may not even be because a rule was breached. Another person may just decide to report your account and if that happens a few times, the account gets suspended.

It is for this reason I say, remove the uncertainty and get your own website. Your website is where you can do your thing. Build it, chop and change it just the way you like; add, tweak, or remove anything with speed and full control.

In general, a website is supposed to do one thing: it needs to tell visitors (and potential customers) exactly what you do and how you can help them go from the situation they find themselves in, to the place they want to go to.

A great website answers the most important questions your prospects have before talking to you face to face. I would go as far as saying visitors decide to talk to you *precisely* because you have answered those questions and shown you already know what they're struggling with.

The more you show you understand your visitors, the easier it becomes for the people who have not seen you anywhere else to trust you. You are basically telling them, *"I get you. I have the solution to your problem. I know so much about you already. I've already helped people just like you, and these are the testimonials they left me. It is safe to stay."*

Structure-wise, there are a few things you cannot go without. They include:

1. Contact details
2. Call to action buttons
3. Mobile responsiveness
4. Fast page load
5. Tracking and Analytics

Let us look at each of these in detail.

Contact details

The contact details on your website (usually a phone number, and an enquiry form) should be easy to find. It is pretty common for websites to display a clickable phone number (otherwise known as click-to-call, more on this later on in the chapter) in the top right corner – although this is not always the case.

Studies have shown that the more prominent the contact details are, the more likely people will get in touch with you. Shocking, right?

Sure, maybe they will not get in touch the first time. Maybe not the second either (remember the 3% rule?). But once they decide that it is time to get in touch, the likelihood they will convert is much higher. All because you made it easy for them.

Call to action buttons

These buttons guide people to the next step of the journey and are supposed to let them know what is going to happen next.

Common sense says that if you do not tell people what you want them to do, they will be unlikely to know what to do, right?

The website is, again, supposed to be built in order to show potential customers what problems you solve and how you can help them get to their desired state in the fastest possible way.

Call to actions are simply there to make it easy for visitors to progress fast through the journey and allow them to make a decision as to whether you're someone who can help them out.

On long form landing pages, where there is a lot going on, you might even have the same call to action repeated three or four times to spare people the need to scroll back up.

Common call to actions marks conversion points like calling a number, filling out a contact form, scheduling a demo, requesting a call back, adding a product to cart, signing up to a webinar or a newsletter, and lots more.

Mobile responsiveness

A website these days needs to be mobile responsive, which means it has to resize and change layout depending on the size of the screen.

Depending on the industry, you usually get between 50% to 95% of your website traffic from mobile phones, so if your website has not been designed with mobile in mind, you are losing a massive amount of a) traffic b) inquiries c) sales.

A suggestion? Go as far as designing primarily for mobile and then adapting for desktop and tablet, not the other way around.

Remember that I just talked about click-to-call numbers? These beauties only work on mobile, because they are essentially a small piece of code that allows visitors to open a mobile number on their keypad when they click on it. Once this number opens, they just have to start the call, instead of having to write down the number, type it on their keypad, and *then* call.

You might think this is not a big deal. But as the genius Steve Krug pointed out in the landmark book on web usability "Don't Make Me Think", and I paraphrase, the more steps you make someone take, the less likely they are to go through with whatever you are asking them to do.

Sure, someone will still call you. But others will not. Why risk it just because you didn't bother to add a tiny piece of code in? Just do it, you'll thank me later.

Fast page load

Otherwise known as, "be as quick as possible to display your website after people click on any of your URLs."

Speed is not only a known ranking factor that Google uses to decide how high (if at all) you are going to show up in the Google search results. It has become a must in the type of fast paced, tech-dominated, internet driven society that we live in we live in.

I am sure that you have' done this yourself. Remember the last time you clicked on a website that did not load in the first 3 to 4 seconds? My bet is you clicked on the back button and went back to whatever you were doing before, because you found that was not a good experience.

See, Google does not like that either. Google wants its users to be happy because happy users mean more advertisers, and more advertisers means more money for Mr. Google. It is, clearly, a win-win-win situation.

Tracking and Analytics

Hand in hand with having a website goes the need to know what your visitors are doing on it. Should be a given, but I cannot tell the number of businesses I spoke with that do not even have basic tracking in place. Why is tracking that important, you might ask?

Through tracking, which is nothing more than some code you place on your website, you are not only able to record specific meaningful actions your visitors take (like submitting a contact form, buying from you, registering for an event and so on) in Google Analytics, but you are also able to categorise those actions by source of traffic.

Which means, you will know if that specific contact form submission, for example, came from Google Search, or Google Ads or a post on your Facebook page, and so on.

Is this infallible? No, it is not. But it gives you a more accurate picture of what channels are giving you the best results over time, which in turn allows you to make strategic decisions around where to spend most of your money and effort.

Having a website that does not track is like flying blind – sure, you are still flying to places, but you never know when you will get knocked out by an invisible obstacle.

Over the years you might have heard a couple of different Google product names being thrown around when it comes to tracking: namely Google Analytics and Google Tag Manager. Briefly, here is what they do and what the differences between the two are.

Google Analytics, as we said, track the visits that come to your website, categorized by source of traffic. In its basic form, Google Analytics will tell you that in the set period you're looking at, 10 people came from Facebook organic, 3 people from Google Ads, 2 people from another referral website, and so on. It is also going to tell you how long they stayed on the website on average, how many pages they visited, and other interesting demographic data.

Google Tag Manager does not record any of that. Google Tag Manager is the middleman that sits in between your website and Google Analytics. Without Google Tag Manager, these two parties would not be able to communicate with each other at a deeper level and share the data that actually allows you to make strategic decisions.

In the simplest possible terms, with Google Tag Manager you give a set of instructions that sounds something like: "Whenever a visitor clicks on button X, send a signal (called tag) to Google Tag Manager, which will then instruct Google Analytics to record that the button was clicked by someone visiting from Facebook."

You can set up a separate tag for each one of the meaningful actions you want to track on your website – whether that is time on page, purchases, inquiries, newsletter signups, add to cart, and more. The possibilities are endless.

This setup, when properly in place, will literally tell you from now until the day you close down your website how many people came from where and what they did.

If you have an e-commerce platform as well, with a little bit more work by your developers you will also be able to attribute the revenue you generated by channel.

Even if you have no intention to run any paid advertising, investing in someone who can set up conversion tracking properly will be priceless for your business moving forward.

Think about how many times in your career you have heard someone say, "I'm not sure how much we got out of this campaign"? This is a great way to reduce that uncertainty to a minimum.

Just to give you a real life example of the difference tracking makes, I have been helping this client of mine who supports nonprofits by writing bespoke grant applications.

She had a website that was already successful. She had consistent traffic. But the problem was that she did not know where those visits were coming from, or what they were doing. Sure, she was getting inquiries, but from where? What should she be doing more of? Where was she wasting her time?

Her goal was to take on more clients for the done-for-you grant writing service, her most profitable activity. If she took on one new client per month, she would have paid for the advertising spend and my fee many times over. I told her that was no problem at all, but before we did that, I needed to set up the tracking.

We concentrated on tracking new business video calls booked through her online calendar, direct inquiries from the grant writing service page, and direct phone calls from ads.

In 3 months, she got 18 new clients and a return on advertising spend in excess of 2,000%. Yes, 3 zeros, that's not a typo.

Is advertising always a smashing success? No, it is not, and I have no problem admitting that. Sometimes a campaign just does not work. In fact, about 80% of all marketing efforts do not work. But the whole point of those marketing efforts is to find the 20% that does.

Sometimes, regardless of how well thought out and structured the advertising campaign is, the results you are looking for just do not materialise. That is usually a sign that the problem lies somewhere else.

This is one of those scenarios in which I turn into the paid ads version of Sherlock Holmes, get my magnifying glass out, and start digging into other areas of the business looking for where you are most likely to be losing the inquiry.

I look at things like:

- Is the website clear enough?
- Is the messaging right?
- Does the website load fast enough?

- Are we tracking everything that we're supposed to?
- Is the tracking actually working?
- How difficult is it to find the contact details?
- Was the landing page built with conversions in mind?

The tricky bit is sticking to the mission and not getting distracted by the sea of data around you. Going down the rabbit hole is way too easy!

5

How to use social media to support advertising

Pretty much every single talk, training or speaking gig of mine will at some point contain the sentence "marketing is an ecosystem", because I wholeheartedly believe that.

There is no such thing as marketing silos anymore. The work of the content team affects social media; the work of SEO affects content; the work of PPC affects SEO; and I could make dozens of other examples.

How well each team does depends largely on how aligned they are with the other teams, and also, how well the marketing department as a whole is in tune with what the business needs.

In previous chapters, I talked about the buyer journey, the importance of making decisions based on data as opposed to feelings, and what a website that will help you convert visitors into inquiries looks like.

Now it is time to talk about the representation of your company (or your personal brand) on social media.

Why am I talking about social media in a book dedicated to paid advertising, you might ask? Believe it or not, the content you share on social media is one of the main factors people take into consideration to help them decide whether they want to buy from you.

While the website is there to show visitors what you do, the problems you solve and the positive change you're going to bring to their life, the social media accounts are where people can, if you are doing things right, get to know you more as human beings.

Hence why, whenever I see a string of dry, uninspiring sales posts, I get annoyed at all those wasted opportunities to connect with customers and prospects on a personal level.

The website is where all that sales talk should be confined to – although if it were down to me, the approach would be consultative rather than sales driven. Just check out

Keenan's bestselling book "Gap Selling" if you are ready to deep dive into that subject.

When people come to me asking what social media platform(s) they should invest in, this tells me that they do not actually know the audience they want to speak to.

It all begins and ends with how well you know who your buyer is. Remember in chapter two, when I spent some time deep diving into the buyer journey? What does the buyer look like? Job role, industry, interests, who and where they hang out?

When you struggle to describe your target customer, it is an indication that you are not ready to run ads. The reason being, if you do not know who you are talking to, you also do not know what problems they have and what questions they need answering; in turn meaning you are not able to say anything that will catch their attention and get them interested enough to check your website out.

Using myself as an example, I know the people I am interested to connect with are on LinkedIn. Lawyers, accountants, finance people, engineers, marketing agency owners all hang out on LinkedIn to learn new stuff, keep up to date with industry news and network with peers. So, there I am too, providing value, educating out on paid advertising (a little) and sharing about my life (a lot). Connect with me if you have not already, by the way? You will find my social media handles at the end of this book.

I am also present on Instagram, but that presence showed me I attract lots of people looking for free information to start their own business, stay at home mums looking for ways to promote their network marketing business, and one-man bands who do not need paid advertising. Not really worth it, so I limit myself to adding a couple of educational posts per month for brand awareness more than anything else.

It is extremely unlikely to find your target market on every platform, and If I am honest, I do not necessarily think having a presence everywhere is a good strategy. Especially considering that 9 times out of 10, when I ask a business what is the goal of being on a specific platform, the answer is a variation of either a) we just have to be on social media; b) we do what our manager tells us to do; or c) we do not really have a goal.

Another problem of spreading yourself too thin is that it gets extremely time consuming to manage your social media presence, and unless the marketing department is on the ball, it's hard to prove what positive impact social media had on the business. *Especially* if upper management insists in trying to tie social media activity to revenue.

Sorry in advance to all the marketing attribution fanatics reading this, but I am a firm believer that most of the good impact social media has on the business is intangible, and therefore it is likely to also be hard to measure. How do you measure positive sentiment, reputation and trust and tie them conclusively to revenue? Good luck and let me know if you ever find a satisfying answer!

Some businesses still believe that social media is a fad and will not spend any time or resources to build a presence. Others will treat it like a box ticking exercise. Others will try to be on social media for a while because they heard it can get you sales, but when they do not see them rolling in immediately, they abandon their accounts, which is even more damaging than not having any presence at all.

Regardless of the platform you choose the entire point of having a social media presence is to show potential customers as well as existing ones the human side of the business. People are more likely to buy from someone who is not only an expert (that comes first and is non-negotiable), but also likeable, relatable and at times imperfect just as much as they are.

It took me a good few years to grasp the concept that nobody likes a know-it-all, because it makes them feel like they cannot measure up. I genuinely thought I needed to show I was perfect all the time, had all the answers, and showed no sign of weakness. The pure 'fake it until you make it' attitude.

I believed I was being helpful to my clients. In reality, I just looked unrelatable, unapproachable, and customers did not tell me because they did not want to hurt my feelings. They simply started to speak more to my colleagues instead.

The way I use social media now is geared towards giving my connections an insight into my life. At times I celebrate wins, at times I share the losses. I am upfront about the challenges I have, and I share how I deal with them. Sometimes I rant, other days are all about gratefulness and positivity.

This is an example of personal branding, clearly, but it can be applied to company channels too. Starting with showcasing more about your people and less about your products or services is an almost surefire way to attract more engagement. Engagement is not the goal, of course – but it is a gateway to the content being shared with more people, as well as the people they know. There is just something about people that makes them interested in other people, so let us capitalise on that!

Another reason to be active (and consistent) on social media is that the ads you run will be attached to your business page. In most cases, people who are interested enough to click on your ads will be redirected to the landing page of your choosing. However, some of them will instead click on your company name and go to your company page to find out more about you. If the company page is not curated, the content is dated or you are not consistent, they are statistically less likely to do business with you.

Updating your business page does not have to be an everyday thing, but regardless of how frequently you can afford to post, just be consistent. If you can only post once a week, be consistent with that. If it is twice a month, fair enough. Be consistent with that. What you definitely should not do is post every day for two weeks and then forget about social media for a month and half. People do not like that. Your inconsistency is sending the message that you are flaky, so your potential customers will be scared that you might behave the same way with them. Besides, that old content may also leave them wondering if you are still in business – definitely not a good start!

Twice in this book already I have talked about the crucial importance of defining your target audience. I will now go into more detail about how I guide my clients through the process.

I suggest you go through the customers you have at the moment (either by yourself or through your account managers, depending on the size of the company) and map out their demographics so you can see if any particular trend stands out.

Are they male or female? What job roles do they have? Are they concentrated in specific geographical areas? What challenges do they talk about? What things do they ask you to fix but you do not have the capability to at the moment? What questions come up time and time again during the sales process? What other personal information would be relevant to this exercise?

Some businesses do it on a spreadsheet, some others have a wall full of post-its they can group and rearrange to give them the best visual representation of what categories, or conversation topics they have available to put a social media content strategy together.

You might think this exercise is time consuming. Yes, it is. You might think it reduces your customers from people to categories. Yes, it does. But categorisation is the most efficient way to find the best target audience for paid advertising (or marketing in general, for that matter).

With categorisation, you get to understand that if 70 customers out of 100 say they go to see a rugby game at least once a month, for example, there is a decent chance that mentioning rugby in your social media content from time to time will get them to engage with you a lot more than sharing how delighted you are that the new battery you put on the market now lasts 12% longer (no disrespect to battery manufacturers intended).

The categorisation cannot and will not be 100% precise, but once you have this picture in your head, it becomes a lot easier to create content these people relate to.

When you understand your audience, you hook them by constant and relevant interaction, so guess what? The moment you drop something that is business-related, they are now more receptive. Understanding this puts you ahead of the social media pack, as you now understand what your people respond to. (For more in depth talk on this go read "Jab, Jab, Jab, Right Hook" by Gary Vaynerchuk, you will thank me later).

Besides, trial and error with organic social media to see what people are responding to is going to tell you which posts are worth putting money behind to capitalise on the momentum... and that is a paid advertising recommendation worth its weight in gold!

6

How to ace the hiring process and find your long-term partner

When you are a business owner, marketing director or decision maker who has to make or approve strategic hiring decisions, it can be quite a daunting task to hire paid advertising help that will leave you feeling confident that they are going to be an asset to your business rather than yet another problem to manage.

You are looking for someone who knows the ins and outs of the job and can deliver to your expectations, yet at the same time, someone who will reframe those expectations if they are not realistic and guide you through the alternatives you have available.

This is not easy, and I want to help. So in this final chapter, we shall go through the must-knows of hiring a good paid advertising agency, which I affectionately call The Seven Must-Knows Of Not Getting Mugged.

1. How paid advertising agencies get paid.

Extremely important to know, as there might be a few things you do not usually think about that will drive the price up and blindside you.

To begin with, it is common to have one-off fees to pay at the very beginning of the contract, when the advertising agency has to go through the setup stage. This one-off payment usually covers the time spent to review the current situation and make sure: the advertising account is set up properly; Google Analytics goals have been implemented, so it is possible to track conversions; Google Tag Manager fires the tags correctly, which means they can be recorded in Google Analytics or, alternatively, they can be imported into Google Ads.

If the review shows that any of these areas are not working, do not exist altogether or are not tracking what you have indicated as the primary goal to focus on, the agency should either have the skills to step in and fix the problem, or guide your in-house web developers to do that instead.

When it comes to the actual advertising management, the most common way agencies get paid is by charging a monthly management fee. It usually includes:

- Campaigns setup
- Ads creation
- Ad copy improvements
- A and B testing of ads, campaigns, or bidding strategies
- Keywords research
- other ad related overhead costs

The advertising management is usually based on a 12 month rolling contract. This means that for the duration of the contract, you will agree on an advertising budget the agency will spend on your behalf, and for that management work they will get either a percentage of the budget or a flat fee. If the advertising budget increases, so will the management fee, but the important thing is to always put those changes in writing (preferably by amending the contract) to make sure there are no surprises on either side.

Some agencies might separate account management from consultancy, as they are technically two separate services. This depends on the way they structure their pricing and packages. There is no right or wrong approach, the important thing is to be on the same page from the start.

Some agencies might also use a performance-based model instead of a percentage or flat fee model. This model, you guessed it, pays based on the outcome of the campaigns, and is prevalent in B2C, specifically in e-commerce, as it is much easier to tie advertising spend to sales and revenue due to a shorter sales cycle.

Both models usually include a one-off initial payment to set things up, so there is no difference on that front.

It is also important to mention that 100% of the advertising budget goes into advertising. Platforms like Google, Facebook, LinkedIn and the likes require that a business card be attached to the advertising accounts. This means that whenever you reach a spend threshold, the platform will take money directly from that card, so there is no need for the advertising agency to pay any invoice to Google or Facebook.

This is extremely important to understand, because if you get an agency that asks you to pay the management fee and advertising spend upfront for the month, you should know that it will make everybody's life harder, and is generally considered bad practice. If there is a legitimate reason for this request, fair enough, but at least request that they keep the advertising money in a separate bank account to make sure that it doesn't get mixed up with the agency's own money. In the UK, as in many other countries, advertising spend is classed as disbursements, so it would create unnecessary accounting complications, such as the need to prove the entire budget was spent.

2. Beware of guaranteed results claims.

Especially if by results you mean inquiries or sales, remember, there is no such thing as guaranteed results. Whether a person inquires or buys from you, that is not something you have control over. You can influence them to a certain degree, for sure, but ultimately, you cannot force them to do anything.

There is, however, something that agencies should guarantee, and that is they are going to find the highest quality people that show interest (or are in-market) for your product or service.

Common sense says that if we introduce your business to high quality website visitors, they are likely to hang out on your website for longer and they are also more likely to reach out to you, which in turn, will increase the chance you will convert them later down the line.

I know that I have already touched on this, but the customer journey is not as linear as we all would like it to be. There is no 'visitors=sales' equivalence. There is no 'visitors=inquiries' equivalence either. The average exposure before someone inquiries or buys from you is seven times, and these touch points can be literally *anywhere* in the buyer journey. Hence why paid ads are not the magical solution, but rather one of your powerful allies on your way to growth.

Say a person sees one of your ads and visits your website. They are usually in the stage where they are exploring their options and doing some research, so if you have done your job right, your ads are likely to appear on multiple related searches. Now you have planted yourself firmly on their radar. Something else, however, jumps higher in their priority list and searching for a product or service similar to yours takes momentarily the back seat, but you are still on the list. Days go by, sometimes weeks, and once their most immediate problem is solved, they are back on the case. They google your name directly in the search bar, get to your website that way, look around a bit more, then fill out an inquiry form. They will likely do the same for a couple of other competitors. Typical scenario if I have ever seen one.

In this case Google Organic would get the credit for the inquiry (you can call it last-touch attribution, if you like fancy names), but really, there have been multiple touch points that all equally contributed to the visitor making the decision to inquire.

So, can anyone promise that paid ads will definitely generate inquiries or sales? No, they cannot. But can advertising find the highest quality traffic for you to increase that chance? Absolutely.

3. Check your business owns your advertising accounts.

The agency should *never* own your accounts. Your accounts are part of your business assets, and should remain so as long as your business lives and breathes.

I saw with my own eyes agencies that pushed for creating new advertising accounts, despite the business already having existing accounts. I also saw agencies wanting to run ads from their own account without giving the business access to it, not even in read-only mode.

Let me be very clear, both scenarios are disgraceful and are fundamentally against best practices. The moment the agency's own interest supersedes the interest of the client they are supposed to be working for, it should be obvious at that point that you are' in bed with the wrong guys.

Your business should be the one with the highest level of access to the accounts, which means you should be the only party able to add or remove users. You should also have a process in place to lock an agency out of the accounts the moment you legally stop working with them, and retain 100% of the work they have done for you.

For clarity, as long as they are working in your account, the agency has no rights to anything contained in it. If they are trying to withhold anything with the claim they are entitled to take back their work, just know this is *not* how it works and you can instruct the relevant people to challenge this.

4. Get in front of real people, fast.

It is all well and good the agency knows how to create ads, but I think you will agree with me that is the bare minimum, considering they are a paid ads agency.

If you want to check their technical knowledge, there are plenty of questions you can ask to do so, but I would argue the most important reason for meeting them face to face is establishing whether you trust these people, and whether the way you do business aligns.

How do they treat you during the discovery process? Are they focused on understanding your business and your current situation? Do they make difficult concepts easy to understand or use complicated jargon to confuse you? Do they tell you they can help you before they even know what the problem is? Do they keep to their word, and get back to you when they promised to get back to you?

You know you are talking to a potential valuable long term partner if during the first chat they will barely talk about themselves, and instead spend the entire time asking questions. You have won the jackpot if the questions they ask continuously probe and clarify what you are saying.

It is not uncommon that conflicting information comes out during the conversation. Maybe you do not know exactly what you are looking for yet, and this discussion will help you gain more clarity and adjust your goals. After all, if you knew everything about paid ads already, what would be the point of bringing professionals into the picture?

There is a huge difference between an agency that takes your answers at face value and one that probes further to make sure your advertising is aligned with the wider business goals.

The agency that digs further looks at every opportunity available to you, guides you through what is best for the business, can explain the reason behind their suggestions, and ensures that whatever they do is in alignment with your goals.

In short, you can tell they really care.

5. Ask to speak to current customers.

If the agency has nothing to hide, there is no reason to refuse letting you speak to existing customers. Actually, they would probably encourage it. Satisfied customers are the best advertising anyone could ever hope for.

6. Read carefully through the terms and conditions.

Request a copy of the T&C's beforehand so you are not caught by surprise when it is time to sign on the dotted line. At that stage you do not have time for the back and forth discussion along the lines of "you didn't tell me this was included/excluded", hence why checking ahead of time can help you identify earlier when the agency isn't a good fit. Specifically, pay attention to:

Length of the contract. Most contracts are done on a rolling basis. This means that if you do not give notice to terminate the contract following the break clause included in the contract, you will automatically enter a new agreement. Take note of the clause, so that in case you want to leave, you won't forget and miss the deadline.

Spend and fees. The advertising spend and the management fee should be both agreed in writing. Any one-off fees should be also agreed in writing, preferably in a different section, and should include the scope of work, making it explicit that this will not be a recurring payment. Consultancy might either be included in the management fee or charged separately, depending on how the agency decides to structure their services. This, too, should be put in writing to avoid misunderstandings and unnecessary gripe.

If after going through the contract you find anything unclear or a little murky, ask for clarifications and/or to make a few amends. As long as they are reasonable, there is no reason for the agency to refuse.

7. Ask what kind of optimisation will be done in your account.

Different agencies have different approaches to account optimisation, but regardless of the approach, they should be able to tell you exactly what they are doing and how frequently they will do it.

The optimisation work is included in the management fee and covers all the technical activity that needs to be carried out in the account on a monthly basis to make sure progress is being made, whathever progress means to your specific situation. This usually includes, but is not limited to: creating new ads; testing new ad copy; adding/excluding keywords (for Google Search); testing new audiences (for Facebook or LinkedIn); reviewing landing pages; reviewing campaign settings.

When you ask what optimisation approach the agency uses and they fail to answer the question (or gloss over it), that is a huge red flag. If this part is not clear, you do not know what you are supposed to be getting for the money you spend, and if you do not know what you are supposed to be getting, you will not be able to complain later down the line if something has not been done. Know what to expect and you will then be able to hold them accountable in the long run.

If you are hiring a person as a full-time member of staff, the same principles and questions apply, minus the contract part.

Focus your attention on how they approach the interview. You are not looking for someone who is taking whatever little information you give them and reply with definitive answers. They cannot possibly have a definitive answer with such limited understanding of the situation.

Test their capability by using scenarios. For example, you can say something like, "We have created 'Campaign X'. The goal is Y. We're not meeting the goal at the moment. How would you proceed to find out what's the problem and how to fix it?"

If they stay clear from definitive answers and again approach this like detective work, asking questions that get them progressively closer to the truth (much like a game of 'Guess Who?'), you can already tell that they will make for a great hire.

That inquisitive mind is what separates a good from the great; the ones who listen and the ones who do not; the ones who will do only what you tell them to, from the ones who will proactively suggest improvements and will be personally invested in the outcomes.

If the person sitting in front of you has come in with a one-size-fits-all approach you could find in any generic marketing blog, they cannot explain why they recommended what they did, make more assumptions than ask questions, the decision of not hiring them will be already made for you.

Free Bonuses

Thank you for sticking with me until the end of this book. I hope you will be able to take the suggestions I shared and apply them to your business.

In case you might still find it tricky, or you need help figuring out how what I said applies to your business, head over to my website and redeem the two free bonuses that come with buying this book.

Bonus one is a 30-minute one to one coaching call with me, where we will explore and discuss your current situation, and how to get where you would like to be.

Bonus two is access to a private community where I will be sharing regular content that you will not find on my website or on any of my social media accounts, and I will periodically organise Q&As and small mastermind sessions, depending on demand.

Redeem the bonuses at:
https://paidadsschool.com/book-sale/

Simply add a valid email address and your receipt number in the 'How To Claim Your Bonuses' section. Once you submit your information, you will receive a confirmation email, and your bonuses will be emailed to you within 2 business days. Please note all bonus materials are digital — there are no physical products.

Contacts

Here are all the places where you can follow or get in touch with me:

Website
https://paidadsschool.com

LinkedIn
https://www.linkedin.com/in/silviacoletto/

Instagram
https://www.instagram.com/thepaidadsschool

Press Inquiries
https://paidadsschool.com/contact-us/

Printed in Great Britain
by Amazon

71905552R00045